Published by SL Resources, Inc.
A Division of Student Life

© 2010 SL Resources, Inc.

Student Life
Attn: Ministry Resources
2183 Parkway Lake Drive
Birmingham, AL 35226

ISBN-10: 1935040804
ISBN-13: 9781935040804

31 Verses Every Teenager Should Know™

www.studentlife.com
www.31verses.com

Printed in the United States of America

CHARACTER

31 verses

EVERY TEENAGER SHOULD KNOW

TABLE OF CONTENTS

WARNING! What you are about to read contains stories of murder, deception, lying, heroes, heroines, cowards, soldiers, prostitutes, and a peeping tom. But, it also contains stories of grace, redemption, forgiveness, victory, and beating the odds. Interested? They're meant to help you see the character of God through the way He interacted with His people in the Old Testament.

What kind of people did God use to show us His character? You might be surprised. God often didn't use the powerful and the influential. He used shepherds, outcasts, and sinners. God chose ordinary men and women to reveal Himself to the world. The one thing these people had in common was that they were willing to be used by God. God wants to use you, too. The question is, "Are you willing to be used?"

If so, keep reading.

Each of these devotions is meant to tell the story of a different biblical character. Some of them will be familiar to you while others may not. The verse at the beginning of each devotion might differ from the passage in the story, but that's OK. They serve as a good summary of the main point or application of the story. It's exciting to see how the Old Testament and New Testament connect! Be sure to read all of the passages (or the whole book) so you can see the whole story.

When you are finished with this book you will have a better knowledge of biblical characters. More importantly, you will know more about God's character. God wants you to know Him; so, dive in deep and see what God wants to teach you.

Your friend,
Bryan Gill

HOW TO USE

Now that you own this incredible little book, you may be wondering, "What do I do with it?"

Glad you asked. The great thing about this book is that you can use it just about any way you want.

It's not a system. It's a resource that can be used in ways that are as unique and varied as you are.

A few suggestions . . .

THE ONE-MONTH PLAN
On this plan, you'll read one devotion each day for a month. This is a great way to immerse yourself in the Bible for a month-long period. (OK, we realize that every month doesn't have 31 days. But 28 or 30 is close enough to 31, right?) The idea is to cover a lot of information in a short amount of time.

THE SCRIPTURE MEMORY PLAN
The idea behind this plan is to memorize the verse for each day's devotion; you don't move on to the next devotion until you've memorized the Scripture you're on. If you're like most people, this might take you more than one day per devotion. So this plan takes a slower approach.

THE "I'M NO WILLIAM SHAKESPEARE" PLAN
Don't like to write or journal? This plan is for you. . . . Listen, not everyone expresses themselves the same way. If you don't like to express yourself through writing, that's OK. Simply read the devotion for each verse, then read the questions. Think about them. Pray through them. But don't feel as if you have to journal if you don't want to.

THE STRENGTH IN NUMBERS PLAN
God designed humans for interaction. We're social creatures. How cool would it be if you could go through *31: Character* with your friends? Get a group of friends together. Consider agreeing to read five verses each week then meeting to talk about them.

Pretty simple, right? Choose a plan. Or make up your own. But get started already. What are you waiting for?

Then the LORD God said to the woman, "What is this you have done?" The woman said, "The serpent deceived me, and I ate."

GENESIS 3:13

Dictionary.com defines an avatar as, "a graphical image that represents a person, as on the Internet." Avatars can be anything you want them to be. If you want your avatar to have green hair and six eyes, you can do that. If you want your avatar to be an ancient warrior princess, armored from head to toe, you can do that, too. However, the odds are if your avatar is a kung fu warrior princess you aren't telling the truth about yourself. But that's common in the avatar world. People live lives they only dream of. That's OK until you can't tell the difference between what is real and what is fake—the difference between the truth and a lie.

Read Genesis 3:1-13. Everything on earth changed after Adam and Eve's rebellion in the Garden of Eden. Evil entered the world, and deception took over. Satan deceived Eve by twisting the truth of God's command. He led her to question God's good intentions, and she gave in. She lost the distinction between the truth and the lie. Even thousands of years later we still feel the effects of Adam and Eve's decision to believe a lie. We often fall into temptation just like Eve did. We believe the lies Satan tells us.
"It's only one sip."
"No one is looking."
"Everyone else is doing it."
"He would love you if you did this."

It's easy to believe Satan's lies. The best thing to do is to test everything. What does God's Word say about it? What do your parents or youth minister say about it? What does your conscience say about it? When you listen to the Holy Spirit, your conscience is in tune with Him. Don't believe the lies. Live in the truth.

1. Why is it so dangerous to distrust God's goodness in our lives?

2. Are there sins in your life that have become so familiar that you cannot tell the difference between the truth and a lie? How did these sins become so ingrained in your life?

3. Describe in your own words what it means to live in the truth.

VERSE

By faith Abel offered God a better sacrifice than Cain did. By faith he was commended as a righteous man, when God spoke well of his offerings. And by faith he still speaks, even though he is dead.

HEBREWS 11:4

What is your most valuable possession? Think about it for a second. When I was in middle school I would have told you that mine was Nolan Ryan's rookie baseball card. Since I've grown older it's things like my car or my wife's engagement ring. But, even these aren't that valuable when compared to India's multi-billionaire Mukesh Ambani's possessions. For example, he is currently building a 27-story mansion in Mumbai, India for almost 2 billion dollars. Regardless of value, we all have things that are close to our hearts.

Read Genesis 4:1-12. Cain worked in the fields, and Abel worked the livestock. In those days people gave offerings to God to show their devotion to Him. The author of Genesis stated that Cain and Abel gave two very different offerings to God. Abel gave fat portions of his best livestock, and Cain just gave some of the crop he had harvested. God wasn't concerned if the offerings were steak from Abel or sweet potatoes from Cain; God wanted their best as well as a right heart toward Him. Cain didn't give with his best attitude of heart. He showed his evil heart in the way that he killed Abel in jealousy and responded to God with anger (1 John 3:12).

Everything we have—our possessions, our time, our money, our talents—is insignificant and seemingly meaningless when compared to Jesus' gift to us on the cross. Nevertheless, we are called to give our best to God and with right attitudes. We can never out-give God, nor can we give God someone else's best. God has given us His best. We are to give Him back ours!

1. Now, seriously, what is your most valuable possession? How would you feel about giving it away for God?

2. What is a way to give God your best in the following? (How can you use these things for God?)
a. Your time:
b. Your money:
c. Your clothes:
d. Your lunch at school:
e. Your vehicle:

3. Why is it important to give back to God?

verse THREE

If you've never seen sprint boat racing before, it's phenomenal. Picture this: two people sitting next to each other in a glorified aluminum boat only inches from the water. Add a 600 horsepower engine and a racecourse that has between 25 and 30 direction changes. Oh yeah, and the race only lasts 50 seconds. That is sprint boat racing! Sounds like fun, huh?

Here's how it works. The driver steers the boat while the navigator tells the driver where and when to turn. The boat is going so fast, and the turns are so sharp that the driver cannot see the racecourse. His only hope of success is to follow the directions of his navigator. But here's the catch—the boat's engine is so loud that the driver can't hear the directions. The only way the navigator can communicate to the driver is through a series of quick hand motions. If the driver doesn't follow these directions exactly, the boat crashes, and the race is over.

Read Genesis 6:1-22. Long before there was sprint boat racing there was another man and his boat—Noah and the ark. Noah had to follow God's instructions down to the smallest detail, or mankind would not have survived the great flood. God told Noah everything he needed to know, and Noah did it. Noah didn't know what an ark was, and had he never seen rain. He just knew he had to trust God, and he did.

Life can seem like a sprint boat race. Everything around us is so loud that we can't hear the directions. The only one we can rely on is the One sitting next to us. We listen to His instructions by studying His Word. Our responsibility is to obey.

REFLECT

1. When was a time that you had to trust God to guide you when you weren't sure what would happen next?

2. You may not know what God has in store for you ten years down the road, but what can you do to obey Him today?

3. Knowing that all of God's instructions are of vital importance, how can you commit to follow His commands carefully?

4

I know that you can do all things; no plan
of yours can be thwarted.
Job 42:2

When I was young, my dad bought our first ATV (all-terrain vehicle). One of the first times I rode it, I sat behind my dad with my arms wrapped around him. I remember feeling weird at first because I couldn't see where we were going. We shot down roads, jumped over hills, splashed through mud, and tilted on two wheels when going over deep ruts. Through all the crazy places my dad took me on that ATV ride, I felt safe because he was driving. I felt safe knowing that my dad was in control, and he was going to take care of me.

Read Job 1:1-22 and 42:2. Despite his righteous lifestyle, Job had a lot of devastating things happen to him in his life: he lost all of his livestock; all of his children died; and eventually Job lost his health. Job would ultimately question God's choice to allow this suffering, but he concluded that God was in control of all the events in his life. Even the bad ones. Even the scary ones. Job continued to praise God even in his pain. Even though he didn't understand his circumstances, he knew that God remained in control and worthy of praise because His character never changed.

Sometimes Christ-followers say, "Why do bad things happen to good people?" The truth is that bad things happen to everyone—good or bad. It's just a part of life. How we deal with the "bad things" not only shows the world what kind of person we are but also shows the greatness of the God we serve. When "bad things" happen in your life, will you react like Job and trust God or will you curse God? God is always in control and always worthy of our praise.

1. Recall a time when you felt out of control either in a car, a roller coaster or perhaps an ATV? How did you react?

2. What do you think was the hardest thing for Job to go through? Why?

3. Recall a time in your life when tragedy struck.

4. How did you respond to God during your tragedy? How did your response draw people to God?

> By faith Abraham, when called to go to a place
> he would later receive as his inheritance,
> obeyed and went, even though he did not know
> where he was going.

HEBREWS 11:8

Do you know the difference between someone having the potential to be good at something and someone actually being good at something? Their actions make the difference. There was a time when Carrie Underwood was just a face in a very large crowd of *America Idol* contestants. Simon Cowell might have told her that she had potential for a successful career in country music. But today her potential has been fulfilled—she's graduated beyond potential and has actually become successful. The same applies to Peyton Manning. You won't hear *Monday Night Football's* Al Michaels say that Peyton Manning has the potential to be a great quarterback—he's already great. He's fulfilled his potential.

Read Genesis 12:1-4. Faith, like potential, can only be shown through actions. Abraham proved his faith in God in many ways, one of which was leaving his home country and traveling to a foreign land where he knew no one and had no family. Abraham didn't question God but simply and completely obeyed Him. Abraham's obedience to God demonstrated his faith. His actions of faith moved him beyond potential. He acted out his faith.

A lot of people are willing to stand up for Jesus at church camps or at worship services, but how does their life change outside of church? We often promise to obey God but never fulfill that promise with our actions. What good is saying that we are going to be obedient if our actions prove otherwise? What good is so-called "faith" in Christ if we never show our faith by actions? Obedience requires more than words: it requires that we move beyond potential and into action.

REFLECT

1. Take a second to look at your faith in Christ. Do your actions line up with your faith?

2. How can you show your obedience to God today?

3. What parts of your life need to change so your actions will line up with your faith?

VERSE

Do not be anxious about anything, but in everything, by prayer and petition, with thanksgiving, present your requests to God.

PHILIPPIANS 4:6

Think about how God answers prayers. On one hand, there are some prayers that can only be carried out by God—they're supernaturally answered. On the other hand, there are some prayers that God answers through you. For example, thousands of people have prayed for victims of natural disasters. I would be willing to say that some of the same people who prayed also donated their money and time for disaster relief efforts. Get it? By using their resources to bring relief, they helped became an answer to their prayers.

Many times we are the ones that change when we pray. For example, when we pray for our enemies, we usually start to care for them because God changes our own attitudes. God uses prayer to change us and help us notice what He's up to.

Read Genesis 24:1-4, 10-26. Abraham's servant knew that God had a special woman picked out for Isaac and knew that only a special woman would care for a stranger and his camels. He prayed that God would identify Isaac's wife through this situation. Abraham's servant became much more sensitive to finding the woman God chose because he asked God for guidance.

Read Philippians 4:6. When we pray, we are telling God that we're not strong enough to handle the situation before us on our own. Praying helps us surrender ourselves to God's guidance and makes us more aware of what He's doing. When we pray, we can be sure that God will hear us. Sometimes God answers our prayers in a supernatural way; other times, we are part of the answer. When we pray, we change and can be a part of changing the world.

1. Do you pray for your enemies? How does your life change after you prayed for them?

2. What areas or people in your life need prayer?

3. List three things you need to seek God's guidance on.

verse
SEVEN

He provides food for those who fear him;
he remembers his covenant forever.

PSALM 111:5

In 1853, a man ordered a French fry-like dish at a restaurant. The guest then complained that his potatoes were sliced too thickly and sent them back to the chef. With a bit of a temper, the chef sliced a potato as thinly as he possibly could and threw them into the hot grease. He served up these crunchy chips to the unexpected delight of the guest. Although pleasing one another did not motivate their attitudes, their actions resulted in one of the most popular snacks in America.

Read Genesis 29:1–30. Honestly, Jacob's story frustrates me. Jacob works seven years for Rachel only to be duped into marrying Leah, Rachel's older sister. That just doesn't seem right. How could God let one of his children get taken advantage of like that? Jacob definitely had a history of deception in his past, but he held up his end of the promise this time. Even though the situation was unfair, God was still working behind the scenes. Jacob would ultimately be renamed *Israel*, father of the nation through whom Jesus Christ was born. Jacob's sons would become twelve tribes, each with numerous descendants, fulfilling God's promise to Abraham.

Now read Psalm 111:5 again. This verse shows us that God was unfolding a bigger plan than Jacob realized. God was faithful to use Jacob to fulfill His covenant with Abraham despite the deception surrounding his life. We may not always feel like God is in control of our lives, but He is always at work and is always faithful. God can work through situations that we don't understand in order to accomplish a bigger goal. Even through bad attitudes and unfair actions (like responding to criticism with a temper), He can work to bring about something totally unexpected and wonderful (like potato chips).

REFLECT

1. What were your feelings when you read that Jacob married Leah?

2. When was a time you did not understand why something was happening?

3. Looking back, how might God have been using that situation for a bigger goal?

VERSE
VERSE
VERSE

8

The LORD was with Joseph and he prospered, and he lived in the house of his Egyptian master.

Genesis 39:2

Have you ever heard the phrase, "You're never safer than when you're in the middle of God's will"? Students who want to spend their spring breaks or summers doing missions sometimes use this statement to get their parents' permission to go. What do you think about this statement? Do you agree?

Read Genesis 37:12-26. Now read Genesis 39:2, 20-21. I'm sure Joseph didn't jump for joy when his brothers threw him into a deep pit or when they sold him into slavery. There were more unfair events that happened to Joseph between chapters 37 and 40—like when Potiphar's wife falsely accused him of rape. But, God was in control regardless of what was going on in Joseph's life and worked through these circumstances to further His greater purpose. If you read all of Genesis 37-45, you'll get a complete picture of the way God used Joseph's circumstances to ultimately set up Joseph as second in charge of all of Egypt, where he saved his family, who were the beginning of the Israelite people, from severe famine.

When we look at Joseph's life we see that he was a man of integrity and that he trusted God in every dark place of his life. Joseph didn't know the great ending of his story until almost fifteen years after his brothers sold him. Still, he remained faithful to God. He probably didn't feel very safe even though he was in the middle of God's will. He wasn't comfortable, for sure. But Joseph trusted in God and remained faithful to Him. If you ever find yourself in a situation of being hurt undeservedly, you can still trust in God. You can trust that He'll never leave you and is always working for His purpose, even if you don't see it for a while.

1. Why do you stop trusting God when bad things happen?

2. Why should you be hopeful in life even when situations are uncomfortable and challenging?

3. What can you do to reaffirm your trust in God in the middle of situations that you don't understand?

And God said, "I will be with you. And this will
be the sign to you that it is I who have sent
you: When you have brought the people out of
Egypt, you will worship God on this mountain."

EXODUS 3:12

The Maltese Falcon is the world's largest and fastest private sailboat.
Its enormous masts soar 187 feet into the sky, and its length spans 289
feet. It has two 1,800 horsepower engines and a sophisticated computer
system that detects wind speed and other important data. It has a private
gym and a full dining room. Now, imagine this boat without its engines or
sails. Without wind or engines, this vessel's fancy equipment is nothing
more than a floating house. It can't fulfill its purpose without some kind of
power to move it.

Read Exodus 3:1–12 and 6:10–13. We just saw that Joseph saved his
family from a great famine. As a result, Jacob moved his family to Egypt
where they multiplied and became the nation of Israel. The Egyptians
then enslaved the Israelites for about 400 years. God called Moses to lead
His people out of slavery. When Moses asked, "Who am I to lead?" God
assured Moses that He would be with him. Moses needed to learn that
God's plan was never about Moses' abilities; it was always about God's
power. Even though Moses was the one God chose to lead the Israelites
out of Egypt, he was nothing without God. Moses was God's choice not
because Moses was Moses but because God was with Moses.

God created each of us with tremendous gifts and abilities. He created us
with purpose and invites us to be a part of His mission. However, we are
like that luxury yacht without sails or engines when we don't depend on
God to accomplish His purpose in our lives. We can accomplish nothing
without Him, but He can accomplish great things through us. It's our responsibility to seek His guidance and be obedient to Him. Then, we leave
the results to Him.

REFLECT

1. When do you most feel like you are trying to live in your own power as a Christ-follower?

2. How does it make you feel to know that your role is only to obey God—you don't have to do anything else—no matter what?

3. Why is trusting God so difficult?

VERSE

But because my servant Caleb has a different spirit and follows me wholeheartedly, I will bring him into the land he went to, and his descendants will inherit it.

NUMBERS 14:24

10

I love epic battles. David versus Goliath. Spartans versus Persians. Rocky versus that Russian boxer. Batman versus Joker. You get the picture. Everything about epic battles intrigues me: the hype, the setting, the smack-talking, the fanfare, and even the face paint—OK, maybe not the face paint. But what intrigues me the most is that in every epic battle both sides think they can win. At the very least, both sides have sufficient courage to join the battle. That is, unless you consider the Israelites.

Read Numbers 13:26-33. When the Israelites got close to the land that God had promised them, Moses sent twelve spies to check out the land and the people who lived there. Ten of these spies wanted to throw up the white flag and surrender even before they started fighting. The cities were large and guarded well with soldiers and equipment. The people were large, too. Of the twelve spies, only Caleb and Joshua believed God had promised this land and would fight the battles for Israel. Caleb had a heart focused on God. This focus gave him courage in the face of battle. He knew that his enemy was big, but he knew that God was bigger and would be faithful to His promise.

Did Caleb have secret ninja skills? No. He believed that if God promised something, He would stay true to His word. Now read Numbers 14:24. Caleb's spirit pleased God, not his ability. Without hesitation, Caleb was willing to follow God into battle against giants. God used Caleb's faithful spirit and willing heart to encourage a nation. God wants to use us, too. When we are faithful to His calling and trust in His greatness, we will have the courage to obey Him.

1. What would your reaction have been if you were Caleb?

2. How can you know that God will follow through with what He promises?

3. Why is it easy to become focused on distractions instead of focusing on God?

4. How do those distractions influence us to make bad decisions?

verse
ELEVEN

The LORD himself goes before you and will be with you; he will never leave you nor forsake you. Do not be afraid; do not be discouraged.

DEUTERONOMY 31:8

Skydiving. What does that word make you think about? An adrenaline rush? Danger? Fear? Fun? Some people make a sport of skydiving; others want to experience it only once. Either way, one of the most common ways to begin the sport is with tandem jumps. In this method, a jumper and a licensed instructor are connected together and jump at the same time. Pretty much all of the work is done by the instructor; the other person just has to trust the instructor, jump, and enjoy the ride.

Read Deuteronomy 31:1-8 and Joshua 1:1-10. Moses was old and was not allowed to enter the Promised Land; however, God was preparing Joshua to be the one who would lead the Israelites in taking the land. Joshua knew the task before him was scary and seemingly impossible. His first task was to take the entire nation across a large river where great opposition would meet them on the other side. Needless to say, Joshua was a little anxious. That's why God repeatedly reminded Joshua that He would never leave him. Regardless of how impossible the task seemed, God would be the one who fought the battles for Israel and who carried out His plan. Joshua simply had to take some leaps of faith.

God and Joshua's relationship was kind of like a tandem skydiving jump: God knew what He was doing. He was in control. He took care of Joshua. He did all of the work. Joshua trusted God and experienced amazing things as a result. As we go through life, we can be sure that when God calls us to do anything—from moving to another country, to having an uncomfortable conversation with a friend—He is always with us. He never leaves us, and He simply asks for our obedience as He does the work through us.

REFLECT

1. When was a time when you felt all alone? How can you know that you are not alone?

2. What tasks have you ever faced that seemed scary or impossible?

3. Write down three situations when you need to hear these encouraging words from Deuteronomy 31:8 the most.

12

By faith the prostitute Rahab, because she welcomed the spies, was not killed with those who were disobedient.

Hebrews 11:31

I watched my wife train for her first marathon. She would get up at 4:30 every other morning and run for miles. Then, on Saturdays she would run longer distances of ten to twenty miles, eventually reaching the marathon mark of 26.2 miles. When she began training, running more than five miles seemed impossible to her. But she was persistent and devoted in her daily training, and she eventually reached her goal.

Read Joshua 2:1–24 and 6:17–25. The Israelites were getting ready to conquer their first city in the Promised Land. Joshua sent spies to Jericho to get a feel for what they were up against. Rahab had heard about the things God had done for the Israelites and knew that He was the true God. She hid the spies because she believed in Him. Rahab was not perfect. She was, in fact, a prostitute—a lifestyle in direct contradiction to God's standards. But, her actions demonstrated that her belief in God was life-changing. She ultimately became a part of the lineage of Jesus.

Chances are, most of us are not prostitutes like Rahab, but we're still sinful and have our own struggles. We cannot wait until we perfect our lives in order to follow God fully. Just like every marathon is completed one step at a time, so goes our faith in Christ. We obey Him every step of the way, one step at a time. We don't have to be perfect to follow Him, but as we allow Him to work through us each step of the way, we get closer to our goal of becoming more like the character of Christ.

1. How does your life reflect the change that God has made in you?

2. What attitudes in your life keep you from serving God?

3. Is there any guilt in your life that you struggle with? How does it distract you from following God whole-heartedly?

For God did not give us a spirit of timidity, but a spirit of power, of love and of self-discipline.

2 TIMOTHY 1:7

A quick Google search can lead you to numerous stories about various persons saving the life of someone who had fallen into the path of a coming subway train. One subway rescuer was Wesley Autrey, a construction worker and Navy veteran. One day when he was taking his two young daughters home, a stranger fell into the tracks. Autrey immediately jumped off of the platform. He pulled the man between the tracks, using his own body to protect him from the train stopping above them. Autrey said that he didn't feel special—he was just a normal person who did what was right.

Read Judges 6:11-16 and then Judges 7:1-21. The people of Midian had begun oppressing the people of Israel. God chose Gideon to lead the Israelites to defeat their Midianite enemies. Gideon objected to God's call by insisting that he was the most insignificant person that God could find. However, God insisted that He would be with Gideon to defeat the Midianites. Gideon began with only 32,000 soldiers in comparison to the innumerable amount of Midianites; however, God instructed him to send home all but 300 Israelite soldiers. Armed with jars, lanterns, and torches they defeated the powerful Midianite army without a single battle.

Read 2 Timothy 1:7. We tend to put biblical characters on a pedestal, forgetting they were simply normal individuals who surrendered to God's bigger plan. We have been called to surrender as well. Sometimes we think that we have to be "super Christians" in order to do anything real for God. But that's just not true. It's not about us, anyway; it's about how great and amazing God is. Thinking we are useless to God is just a lie! God works through ordinary people—like you and me—to accomplish His work.

1. How did God get more glory by using only a small number of soldiers with Gideon?

2. What reasons do you give God for not being usable by Him?

3. Why are those reasons insufficient?

4. Write a prayer thanking God for His desire to use you as part of His plan.

VERSE

Though you have made me see troubles, many and bitter, you will restore my life again; from the depths of the earth you will again bring me up.

PSALM 71:20

Have you ever watched *The World's Strongest Man* competition? These guys seem to bench press the weight of small countries and tear cars into tiny pieces. You can tell that these dudes are strong just by looking at them. When a guy doesn't have a neck, his arms are as big as pumpkins, and his legs are like tree trunks, there is no secret to where his strength comes from—his muscles.

For years, that is how I pictured Samson, and he may have looked pretty muscular. Still, the Philistines knew that protein shakes weren't his secret to super-strength. Read Judges 13:1-16:31. (Yeah, that's a lot of verses, but don't worry, it's a great story.) Did you notice how many times the author told us that the Spirit of the Lord gave Samson his power? Samson's strength came from God to use for God's glory. Samson, however, had some major character flaws and disobeyed God over and over. Now read Psalm 71:20. This psalm is not specifically referring to Samson, but it illustrates the way that God can restore a relationship broken by sin. Samson realized the real source of his power. He used his strength for the glory of God as he destroyed the pagan worship of idols.

God gives us gifts and abilities to use for His glory. Sometimes we forget that these gifts are not for ourselves but to use for Him. He always stands ready to redeem us from our shortcomings and let us be a part of His plan. Despite Samson's disobedience, we must remember that God was gracious to Samson and allowed him to be the final instrument in defeating the Philistines. God promises to use us in spite of our failures when we turn to Him.

1. Why do you think God chose Samson to defeat an entire nation?

2. How have you considered using your gifts and abilities for God? How can you use them for Him instead of yourself?

3. In what ways do you need God to restore your relationship with Him?

verse

FIFTEEN

The women living there said, "Naomi has
a son." And they named him Obed. He was
the father of Jesse, the father of David.

RUTH 4:17

The world's largest commercial jigsaw puzzle has 24,000 pieces. It is entitled *LIFE: The Great Challenge* by Royce B. McClure. It's over 14 feet long and 5 feet high. When completely assembled, it's a beautiful collage of an ocean scene, outer space, animals, sailboats, and hot air balloons. What if you were to work for weeks or months putting this puzzle together only to realize that there was one piece missing? It would be devastating to find out that you had an incomplete picture.

Read Ruth 1-4. Ruth may seem like a strange, Old Testament love story that we don't understand well. But Ruth's story is a great example of God's sovereignty. Israelites despised Moabites and their culture. So for Ruth, a Moabite woman, to remain faithful to Naomi and move with her to Israel was a big step of faith. But Ruth was faithful to follow God, and she became a part of the Israelite people. God providentially cared for Ruth through Boaz, and His perfect plan unfolded in their marriage. They had a son named Obed, who was the grandfather of King David. Jesus came through this same lineage. Ruth is a vital piece in the genealogy of Jesus! She probably never imagined her importance when she came to Israel as a despised Moabite!

Pay close attention to Ruth 4:17. Ruth may have thought her life was an incomplete puzzle. I'm sure, at the time, she didn't know how she would fit into the greater scheme of God's plan. Nevertheless, she was stubbornly faithful to Naomi and trusted God at all times. Like Ruth, we often may not understand how God is using us. We can be encouraged that when we are faithful to Him, we can trust that He is working to use us as part of His complete and finished plan.

REFLECT

1. How do you respond to God when you don't understand your circumstances?

2. Why can you trust God to use you as part of His plan, even when you aren't sure how He's working?

3. How do you want God to use your life to help others?

16

There is no one holy like the LORD;
there is no one besides you; there is
no Rock like our God.

1 Samuel 2:2

The movie *Rudy* was inspired by the true story of Daniel "Rudy" Ruettiger. Rudy aspired to play football for the University of Notre Dame but didn't possess the ability, size, or grades to be accepted into the university. He received multiple rejection letters from Notre Dame. In a moment of frustration, he went to visit Father Cavanaugh, a priest who had advised and befriended him. Rudy stated, "Maybe I haven't prayed enough." Father Cavanaugh replied, "I'm sure that's not the problem. Praying is something we do in our time. The answers come in God's time."

Read 1 Samuel 1:1-2:11. Hannah desperately wanted a child and prayed continually for one. Year after year, Hannah's prayers were unanswered. To add to the problem, Peninnah cruelly teased Hannah about not being able to have children. We don't know if Hannah was ever upset with God, but we do know that she was upset about the situation. Ultimately, God answered her prayers and blessed her with what she desired the most—a son. Hannah named her son Samuel, and she devoted him to God by giving him to Eli, the priest, to raise as a servant for God.

Our prayers are often answered in ways that we don't understand. Sometimes we pray for good things, and they don't happen; sometimes we pray against bad things, and they do happen. Does that mean that God ignored our prayers or doesn't love us? No. Does that mean that we didn't pray hard enough? No. Sometimes God answers in ways that we have to wait for, and sometimes He answers in ways that we will never fully understand. No matter what, our role is to trust God that He will answer our prayers in His timing and in His way. We pray as determined children of God and leave the answers to "come in God's time."

1. Why is it difficult to not receive what we ask for immediately?

2. How do you expect God to answer your prayers? Do His answers change who He is? Do His answers change how you feel about Him?

3. Why can you trust God no matter what His answer to your prayer may be?

4. What can you do while you are waiting for an answer from God?

And the boy Samuel continued to grow in stature
and in favor with the LORD and with men.
1 SAMUEL 2:26

What do the following people have in common: Mozart, Alexander the Great, and Michael Jackson? Anybody know? OK, here's the answer: they all did amazing things at a young age. Mozart composed his first symphony at about five years old. Alexander the Great was fourteen when he started conquering countries. Michael Jackson was six years old when he sang as lead singer of *Jackson 5*. These are just a few examples of countless people in history who made an impact at an early age.

Read 1 Samuel 2:18–21, 26, and 3:1–20. Remember: Samuel was raised in the Temple, helping Eli—not close to the Temple, IN the Temple. Samuel was obedient to God and grew in his relationship with Him. When God first called Samuel as a prophet, he had already been faithful to live according to God's Word. He then began a very personal relationship with God as His prophet—the one who relayed the word of God to the people. Samuel was faithful to God's words, and all of his prophecies were true. As a result, all of Israel recognized God's calling on his life.

God has called us to give ourselves completely to Him at all times. We don't have to wait until we're at a different place in life to follow Him intently. The good news is that we don't have to miss out on life to follow God; we can make an impact for Him now! He wants to be central in everything we do. When He becomes our focus, everything we do is significant because our lives are for His glory.

1. How can you overcome fear when God calls you to do something you don't feel ready for?

2. What kinds of things do you feel you have to wait until you are older to do for God?

3. What is most holding you back from following God wholeheartedly now?

4. What is one thing that God is calling you to do now?

VERSE 18

Have you ever met someone and then almost immediately forgot his or her name. What happens the next time? You're supposed to know that person; maybe you begin calling him or her by the wrong name. But, no matter how sincere you are, no matter what your intentions are, you are still using the wrong name. Nothing can save you from embarrassment at this point.

Read 1 Samuel 13:6–14 and 15:10–11, 26. The people of Israel had asked for a king. In doing so, they were essentially rejecting God as their one true King. However, God provided guidelines for an earthly ruler and instructed Samuel to anoint Saul as the first king. At first, Saul was eager to follow the directions of God through Samuel. Before long, though, Saul thought his way was better than God's way. Saul's act of offering a sacrifice was not bad in itself, but his actions were in direct disobedience to God's instructions (given through Samuel) to wait for Samuel to offer the sacrifice. Because Saul did not obey, God stripped his kingship from him. God wanted someone who would seek God above anything and everybody else.

Sometimes we think that as long as we're doing something "good" God will bless our actions. No matter how sincere we are, if those actions are against His calling or commandments, we aren't doing what He wants. God wants our full obedience to His commands, not what we think or want to be His commands. Like calling someone the wrong name, when we are wrong, we are just wrong. We can't change God's instructions any better than we could change a person's name by using a different one. God is looking for someone to follow His plans—not his or her own. Are you that person?

REFLECT

1. Describe a time when you tried to do things your own way and it didn't work out for you.

2. Why do you think people try and do things without God's help?

3. In what ways do you try to develop your own agenda for God instead of following His plan for you?

> Then Davaid said to Nathan, "I have sinned against the LORD."
> Nathan replied, "The LORD has taken away your sin.
> You are not going to die."
> 2 SAMUEL 12:13

The American poet, Ralph Waldo Emerson wrote "Concord Hymn", describing the beginning of the American Revolutionary War that occurred on April 19, 1775 in Concord, Massachusetts. There is a famous line in the opening stanza that is still used today to describe the impact of that night. The lines read,

> *Here once the embattled farmers stood,*
> *And fired the shot heard 'round the world.*

A single gunshot by itself may seem to be insignificant, but this shot started a war. That shot affected the freedom of the colonies then and even us today. Its effect was more far-reaching than the gunman could have ever realized.

Read 2 Samuel 11:1-27 and 12:1-18. This story seems to begin with a single look. But even before that look, the author wanted readers to see the contradiction in where David's leadership responsibilities were and what he was actually doing. Instead of going to battle with his soldiers, he was spending some leisure time at his palace. He was at the wrong place, at the wrong time, allowing a single look (perhaps even an unintended one) at a woman to lead him into sins including adultery, deception, and murder.

We often justify "one little sin" by thinking that it's insignificant. Our sins may seem insignificant, but their consequences reach far beyond the initial action. We can see from David's life that his disregard for his responsibilities ended up greatly affecting the lives of numerous people. Worst of all, David hurt his relationship with God. Fortunately, we also see that David ultimately understood how great his sin was and repented to God. Because of His grace and mercy, God restored the relationship. The consequences of David's actions were not taken away, but God's mercy to David provided a renewed relationship.

REFLECT

1. What does this story teach us about the significance of our actions?

2. How could this chain of events have been avoided?

3. How have your sins affected those around you? How have the sins of others affected you?

4. Why is sin so dangerous?

20

So Solomon did evil in the eyes of the LORD; he did not follow the LORD completely, as David his father had done.

1 Kings 11:6

What is the one thing that can defeat Superman? Exactly—kryptonite. It weakens him and makes him vulnerable to pain and suffering— even death. Evil villains can't defeat Superman with bullets. They can't overpower him with ropes or chains. Why? The answer is simple: those weapons aren't effective. But Superman has to watch out when a malicious mastermind like Lex Luthor gets his hands on some kryptonite. With kryptonite nearby, Superman's weakness allows the evil villain to gain power over him.

Read 1 Kings 3:5-15, 10:23-25 and 11:1-13. When Solomon became King of Israel, he asked God for wisdom and discernment in knowing how to rule the people. God granted this request and made him the wisest king in the world. God blessed his power, land, and wealth beyond imagination. He was superior to nearly every king that came before or after him. But Solomon filled his life with 700 wives and even more concubines who didn't worship God. God warned the Israelites about the dangers of marrying these women and commanded against it. Solomon disobeyed, and his wives led him away from the true God and to worship their false gods. His wives became the kryptonite to his greatness.

We all have our own form of kryptonite that Satan uses to make us stumble. For some it may be power. For others it may be money. It might be gossip, lying, lust, food, or laziness. Whatever temptation we face, Satan knows how to weaken us. Some temptations we can avoid altogether. If Solomon would have obeyed God in the first place, he could have avoided the temptation to follow other gods altogether. Other temptations we can't avoid, and we must use God's Word as our guard against sinning in the face of temptation. In all situations, when God's Word is central in our lives, we allow Him to direct us away from sin and temptation.

1. What is the "kryptonite" in your own life?

2. How has Satan used this to make you stumble?

3. How can you guard yourself against these attacks in the future?

VERSE 21

Trust in the LORD with all your heart and lean not on your own understanding; in all your ways acknowledge him, and he will make your paths straight.

PROVERBS 3:5-6

When I took my first ministry position out of seminary, my wife and I didn't have much money. We had several bills to pay, but I hadn't received a paycheck yet. The bills would cost $130 more than we could pay. My wife and I prayed for God to give us wisdom. The next morning God reminded me about a bag of clothes we were going to sell. My wife took that bag to the consignment store to see if she could sell them. They gave us $134 for the clothes! God had provided enough for us to pay our bills and have a little left over for a cheeseburger.

Read 1 Kings 17:1-16. Elijah was battling the people of Canaan and their false worship of Baal. The Canaanites attributed rain to the life cycle of Baal. During the rainy season, he was living; during the dry season, he was dead. Sounds weird, right? God wanted the Canaanites to know that He controlled the rain; He demonstrated it by bringing a drought. . The resulting famine forced Elijah to trust God alone to provide him with food. God had plans for Elijah's life and gave him exactly what he needed to accomplish His purposes and plans.

The way that God provided for Elijah was unconventional, to say the least. If Elijah had relied on his own abilities to provide for food, he likely would have failed. God is in charge of all things, though, and was able to provide in ways that Elijah could not have imagined. We will face tough times in this life. But when God calls us to follow Him, He also promises to give us what we need to accomplish His work. We can follow Him with great assurance that He will provide whatever we need to fulfill His plan!

REFLECT

1. When have you seen God's provision in your life?

2. Why is it difficult to trust God in tough times?

3. What are some ways that you can miss or ignore God's provision in your life?

VERSE

When they had crossed, Elijah said to Elisha, "Tell me, what can I do for you before I am taken from you?" "Let me inherit a double portion of your spirit," Elisha replied.

2 KINGS 2:9

When I was in middle school, one of the best players on the high school football team was my hero. He was about six years older than I was, and I looked up to him for several reasons. He was an awesome high school football player: he was big, fast, and strong. More importantly, he was a devoted Christ-follower. He won an award at his senior sports banquet honoring his commitment to Christ both on and off the field. I had seen that award alongside his other awards and thought, "I hope I'm like this guy one day."

Read 2 Kings 2:1-18. Elijah's time as God's prophet was coming to a close, and Elisha was his successor. Elisha closely followed Elijah on the day he was to leave earth, respectfully unwilling to leave him or God's calling. Just before God picked up Elijah in the chariots of fire, he asked Elisha what he wanted from him. Elisha didn't say, "I want your fame," or "I want your power." He said, "I want a double portion of your spirit." He wanted the same spiritual power. Although it may sound a bit selfish, His request actually was similar to one that a first-born son would ask of his inheritance from his father. God answered this request, and Elisha carried on in Elijah's place.

Elisha knew that he was unfit to live the life of a prophet of God by himself. So, he asked for help from his "hero." When God has called us to do anything, we must remember that we are ineffective in our own power. However, God's power will see us through to the completion of His plan. Remember, God will give us what we need to do His work. He will equip us with the tools to make His name known.

1. Who are the spiritual mentors or heroes in your life?

2. What is God calling you to do and how is he equipping you to do it?

3. How has God provided with what you need to be a part of His plan?

verse
TWENTY-THREE

The Dog Whisperer, Cesar Millan, has an incredible skill. He knows how to help unruly dogs become the world's best dogs and can teach dog owners to become somewhat like a dog whisperer themselves. He can silence lapdogs and stop pit bulls in their tracks with a sound or hand gesture. He urges dog owners to reward good behavior (with praise or affection) and discipline unwanted behavior (with a gentle physical or verbal correction). It's pretty amazing to watch.

Read Hosea 1:1-3, 3:1-5. God gave Hosea, a prophet, the unusual command to marry Gomer, a prostitute. As expected, Gomer was not faithful to Hosea. But, God told him to love her and to keep pursuing a relationship with her. One time, he even had to buy his wife out of a type of slavery because she left him! Hosea, however, was faithful to obey God's command to redeem her. Hosea's life with Gomer was a picture for Israel to see their spiritual adultery against God. God chose Israel to be His people. They were consistently unfaithful to Him in their worship of other gods. But God loved them anyway and constantly pursued them for redemption, ultimately providing complete redemption through Jesus.

Sometimes we picture God as "The Heavenly Dog Whisperer" whose purpose is to control our behavior with rewards or discipline. But we are not His pets; we are His chosen family. Although God is just and our sin is punishable by death, Jesus took our punishment on the cross. He desires to restore us despite our sin and does so through Christ. We can be confident that God loves us even when we mess up. He wants to forgive. He wants to redeem. He wants to restore. So, we can turn to Him with confidence that He loves us and wants us.

REFLECT

1. How would you have reacted if you were Hosea, and God told you to marry Gomer?

2. How do you act toward God when you sin?

3. How does it make you feel to know that God wants to forgive you—that He's not hoping you'll make a mistake so He can punish you?

4. Write a short prayer confessing your sins and thanking God for forgiving you and loving you.

24

> Then I heard the voice of the Lord saying, "Whom shall I send? And who will go for us?" And I said, "Here am I. Send me!" Isaiah 6:8

The Louvre Museum in Paris, France is one of the most famous museums in the world and also the largest at nearly 645,800 square feet. It displays over 30,000 pieces of art including da Vinci's famous Mona Lisa. Much of it used to be a palace, so you can imagine the beautiful details of the French building itself. Imagine walking through the middle of the museum, soaking in each masterpiece. Now, imagine that the power goes out. It's completely dark. There's not a bit of light anywhere. What can you see now? Nothing—because you are walking around in the dark. You can't see what's around you because you are far from the light.

Read Isaiah 6:1-8. Isaiah's calling as God's prophet was an out-of-this-world event. He saw the Lord sitting on His throne, being praised continually by angels with six wings. Immediately Isaiah realized his sinfulness in front of a holy God and confessed his sin. God forgave Isaiah and declared him forgiven. Then, when the Lord asked whom He could send to do His work, Isaiah spoke up and said, "Here am I. Send me!" Can you picture the scene? God's beauty and majesty revealed Isaiah's true person. In response, Isaiah could do nothing but give his life to the one true God who could redeem him.

Our relationship with the holy God reveals the sin in our lives by the illuminating holiness of God. When we are close to the Light, our true nature is revealed. When we're confronted with the awesomeness of God, we give our lives to Him in service. Like the lights in the Louvre, being close to the source of holiness allows us to see the beauty and holiness that we are to reflect through our lives.

1. How would you describe your fellowship with God?

2. Looking back on your life, describe a time when you felt closest to God. How did you feel? How did others see you? What were you doing differently than you're doing now?

3. How does an accurate view of yourself before a holy God help you to depend on Him more?

Do not merely listen to the word, and so deceive yourselves. Do what it says.
JAMES 1:22

Have you ever wished bad things on somebody else? What about that car that drives closely behind you for miles? Or that person at school or church who has treated you like garbage? Or that teacher who has been unfair? Or that family member who hurt you? It's so easy to want retribution. None of these people have done anything to deserve grace, right? So, why do you have to obey God's command to love them like you love yourself? Because He's God, and we have the responsibility to honor Him and reflect His love to the world.

Read Jonah 1:1-12, 1:17, 2:10, 3:3 and 3:10-4:3. (Or for a good story take a few extra minutes and read the whole book. Go ahead; it's pretty short.) God gave Jonah very clear and specific instructions: "Go to the great city of Nineveh and preach against it." The Ninevites were wicked, evil people, but what did Jonah do? He went the other direction and found himself in the belly of a big fish. Jonah wasn't confused about God's instructions; he deliberately disobeyed them.

When Jonah finally obeyed God and went to Nineveh, God changed the hearts of that great city, and they were sorry for their wickedness. This should have made Jonah happy, right? Well, it didn't. He wanted them to receive punishment for their wickedness. Jonah didn't agree with what God wanted to do because he thought the Ninevites didn't deserve forgiveness. However, that was not for Jonah to decide. God's commands are not meant to be ignored simply because we don't understand or don't agree with Him. God gives us instructions, and we leave the results to Him. Our responsibility is to do what God tells us and trust God with the rest.

1. What is one thing that God has told you to do, but you haven't done yet?

2. Do you ever approach God as an authority figure who you want to rebel against? Why or why not?

3. How would your responses to God change by thinking of Him as a loving God who has your best interest at heart?

VERSE

But seek first his kingdom and his righteousness, and all these things will be given to you as well.

MATTHEW 6:33

26

OK, it's experiment time. Grab a one-gallon, wide-mouthed jar; a dozen fist-sized rocks; a bucket of gravel; a bucket of sand; and a pitcher of water. Got it? Probably not, but imagine with me anyway. At first thought, it seems like they won't fit into the same jar, but you'd be surprised at the result. You see, if you put the big rocks in first, the small things will fit; however, if you put the small things in first, the big rocks won't fit. That's kinda how it is with life. Make sure the most important thing in your life (God) is given first priority. If He is put last (just like the big rocks) there isn't any space for Him.

Read 2 Chronicles 34:1–7. King Josiah became king when he was eight years old. Eight years old! The author of 2 Chronicles said that although the kings before him had led Israel away from God, Josiah did what was right in the eyes of the Lord. By the time he was the age of 16, he wanted to seek God fully; it was only after seeking God that Josiah's reign started to make a significant impact. After seeking God, he was confronted with the sinfulness of Israel's idol worship. He tore down the altars of Baals and smashed all of the idols and carved images in an effort to get rid of all wickedness in the nation.

Everything fell into place in Josiah's life after he sought God's direction and guidance. Seeking God allowed him to recognize sin and reorder the priorities of Israel so that they were following God once again. When we seek God above all things, we want to live according to His desires because we see the uselessness of following after anything else. When we put God first, like the big rocks in our experiment, we make sure that our most important thing takes priority.

1. What "big rocks" in your life are you ignoring?

2. How would your life look if God were your first priority? What are some things in your life that take priority over God?

3. What are some practical ways to put God first in your life?

verse
TWENTY-SEVEN

Then the LORD reached out his hand and touched my mouth and said to me, "Now, I have put my words in your mouth."

JEREMIAH 1:9

Most people picture boys' locker rooms as smelly places with dirty socks draped over the benches and strange creatures lurking in the corners. Even with the overuse of deodorant spray, the smell doesn't go away. In fact, that smell is probably worse than you are imagining. Even with all the grossness that makes up a locker room, that stuff is not the worst part. The locker room is where guys like to brag about all the bad stuff they've done. They try and see who has the wildest story about getting wasted, hooking up, or putting others down. It's not popular to be the "good guy." You're going to get made fun of.

Read Jeremiah 1:4-10 and 20:1-18. Jeremiah was the kind of guy who would stand up for God under any circumstances. God called him to be a prophet to the nations. Jeremiah had to tell the people everything that they were doing wrong in God's eyes. As you can guess, that didn't make him the most popular prophet in town. But Jeremiah's love for God compelled him to speak so that God's words were like fire inside him. In other words, Jeremiah couldn't keep from speaking. Regardless of how much people ridiculed him, Jeremiah's faithfulness was stronger than his fear of other people.

It's difficult to follow Christ. I mean, we all want to fit in and be liked by people. But sometimes, fitting in requires us to compromise our commitment to God, and that compromise is a trap of sinful behavior. Standing firm in our beliefs and convictions isn't easy when we live in a culture that expects us to give in to temptation. God calls us to be faithful to follow Him, even when we are surrounded by others who want to pull us into the smelly corners of temptation.

REFLECT

1. What is the most challenging thing about following Christ?

2. How does God want you to respond when people insult you because of your faith?

3. When was a time you felt like you couldn't keep from telling somebody about Jesus?

28

Now when Daniel learned that the decree had been published, he went home to his upstairs room where the windows opened toward Jerusalem. Three times a day he got down on his knees and prayed, giving thanks to his God, just as he had done before. **Daniel 6:10**

I've always wanted to go shark diving in a cage. It looks like fun to me! Have you ever wondered what the first conversation about testing shark cages sounded like?

"We're going to need you to test this cage for us."
"That's cool. Why do you need to test it?"
"Um…We need to see if it will work in the water."
"Why would you need a cage in the water?"
"Umm…Jump in and you'll find out."
SPLASH (cue *Jaws* theme music)

The thing about being in shark-infested waters is that as long as someone feels protected by the cage, he or she is willing to go in the water. Without a cage, that person would likely have a change of heart.

Read Daniel 6:1-23. Daniel was a devoted man of God. When the king decreed that prayers and worship could only be offered to the king himself, Daniel prayed to God anyway. His continued faith in God led to some serious consequences. He knew that he would face death in the lions' den but trusted in God to deliver him. When Daniel was thrown into the den, God shut the mouths of the lions. Without God's protection, Daniel would have been a tasty treat. Yet, even if God had not saved Daniel from death, he was willing to be faithful to Him.

It's easy to follow Christ when everyone around us is supportive and encouraging. When it's safe to follow Him, we feel like we have a cage of protection around us. However, standing on our convictions when it may cost us is not as easy. Like Daniel, God has called us to remain faithful to Him no matter what our circumstances look like or how uncomfortable we feel. He is bigger than anything we can face, and He is worthy of our constant faithfulness.

1. Describe a time when you have been persecuted for your faith? How did you respond?

2. When are you most uncomfortable as a Christ-follower?

3. How has God shown Himself faithful to you? How have you shown faithfulness to God?

> And who knows but that you have come to royal position for such a time as this?

ESTHER 4:14B

Here's the rundown on football: there are 11 players on offense and 11 players on defense. Each player has a different role: the running back has a different role than the quarterback, and the wide receiver has a different role than the center (the guy who hikes the ball to the quarterback). Each player has to know his role and do it the best he can. Some positions seem to be more prestigious than others, but football is a team sport—every player is necessary. Running backs wouldn't be successful without an offensive line to block defenders, and wide receivers wouldn't have a ball to catch without a quarterback to throw it to them.

Read Esther 4:1-5:3. Esther was a Jew but lived in a time when Israel had been exiled to another land—at this time, under the control of Persia. Through a series of events, Esther won favor with the King of Persia and became queen. An advisor of King Xerxes, Haman, was seeking revenge against one of the Jews and sought a way to ensure the death of all Jews. The king was unaware that his new queen was a Jew and was tricked into issuing a the decree to kill all of them. Esther arranged for a way to beg the king to save the lives of her people, which he granted (and punished Haman instead). Because of her boldness, a whole nation was saved. Esther knew that God had made her queen for a reason. She fulfilled her role.

God has a role for you where you are as well. You can bring God glory where He has placed you and in the circumstances you live in. Whether it's on your sports team, your band, or your club, God has something He wants to accomplish through you. How will you make yourself available to be used by Him?

1. Where might you be strategically placed by God in your life?

2. What areas of your life have you not made available to be used by God?

3. How can you use the gifts God has given you and the role you've been given to glorify God?

VERSE

30

If the world hates you, keep in mind
that it hated me first.
JOHN 15:18

Rubber band wars are fun. The trick is to use the correct amount of resistance to make it go the desired distance. A little resistance will keep the rubber band closer, but pull it back as far as you can, and it'll go a long way. When you think about it, the only way to use rubber bands is to stretch them. Rubber bands remind me of committed Christ-followers. All believers will be "stretched" at some point in time, whether through challenging circumstances or persecution. Scripture is clear that followers of Christ cannot avoid persecution.

Read Nehemiah 4:1-23. Nehemiah lived during the time of Jewish exile in Persia. The king allowed some exiles to return to Jerusalem, and they rebuilt the Temple. Years later, Nehemiah was concerned for God's image as His city lay in ruins, so he asked the king for permission to rebuild the city's protective walls. With Jerusalem's walls in shambles, the surrounding nations would view God as unable to provide security for His people. When Nehemiah and his workers began the project, they experienced great persecution and danger. The persecution didn't stop them; in fact, it made them more committed to the task. They completed the task in spite of enormous opposition.

The Enemy uses persecution in an effort to stop us from doing God's work. Jesus experienced persecution, and He explained that it would be no different for us. God has not promised us that we will be free from persecution. In fact, Jesus promises the exact opposite. But He tells us that He will be with us as we share in His suffering. We won't be able to avoid being stretched as Christ-followers, but we can take heart that we are following in the footsteps of Christ, and He has promised to be with us through it all.

1. What is your first reaction to persecution?

2. How should we respond to people who persecute us?

3. How can our persecution be a witness for Christ?

4. How can we grow spiritually through persecution?

For the word of the LORD is right and
true; he is faithful in all he does.
PSALM 33:4

Everyone in my family is pretty clumsy. When we see someone stumble,
we joke that they must be related to us. But how do you really know who
someone is? Is it by their looks, their name, or their mannerisms? Is it
by their actions? Perhaps it's by all of these ways, but the way a person
acts says more about him or her than anything else. The things people
do tell us who they are. The same is true with God. What God does in and
through people tells us who He is.

Read Psalm 33:4. God revealed Himself to individuals throughout history to show us more about who He is, and He has shown Himself to be
faithful. He used all the characters we studied in this devotional book to
accomplish this goal. These Bible stories are true, and they all reveal
a different aspect of the character of God. We learn more about God
by seeing the way He interacts with His people and the commands He
gave them. Each person in the previous 30 devotions is different; the only
common denominator is that God was with him or her, and He used each
for His purposes.

We can confidently place our faith in the truthfulness of the Word of
God. When we spend time in His Word, we discover who He is because
He has revealed Himself through His actions as recorded in Scripture
and the commands that He gives us. We must remember, though, that
God's ultimate revelation of Himself came in the man of Jesus. When
we know Jesus, we know more of God, and the Word of God is central
to knowing both.

REFLECT

1. What has God taught you about Himself through this book?

2. How does knowing Jesus show you more about the character of God?

3. What commitment can you make to know God better by spending time in His Word?

CLOSING

Congratulations! Jump for joy! Bring out the piñata! You did it! You finished the book. I hope you learned a lot about God's character from these passages. We serve a pretty amazing God, don't we?!

If you read carefully then you saw that God used some pretty ordinary characters to accomplish His work. Could you relate to any of those stories? Have you struggled in some of the same ways that God's heroes and heroines struggled? Hopefully you were challenged. Hopefully you've been encouraged. Above all, hopefully you've been changed. Whatever your reaction, I hope you finish this book with a sense of awe and wonder at how amazing God is!

There are many more characters in the Bible than just what you've read about in these pages. There may have been some you thought we left out; that's because we did. We couldn't fit every character into a *31 Verses* book. The others are still out there for you to discover and rediscover again and again. God's complete character cannot be described to you in these short pages. So pick up your Bible and start digging away. There is a whole world out there of biblical characters just waiting to be discovered. There's one about some guys walking around in a fiery furnace; there's one about two bears eating teenagers, and we've not even gotten to the New Testament yet. So, keep reading and growing in your relationship with God!

about the

author

BRYAN GILL and his wife, Sarah, live in Memphis, Tennessee with their Yellow Lab, Roscoe. Bryan graduated from Auburn University with a B.A. in Communication and from Samford University's Beeson Divinity School with a Master of Divinity. Bryan is the Baptist Collegiate Ministry director for Metro Memphis. Basically, he gets to hang out with college students for a living. Bryan is an avid photographer and loves Playstation 2. He met Sarah at Auburn University, and they've been married since 2006. Sarah's identical twin sister married Bryan's best friend from high school two weeks after Bryan and Sarah's wedding.

EXECUTIVE EDITORS
Jeremy Maxfield
Jenny Riddle

CONTRIBUTING EDITOR
Andy Blanks

COPY EDITOR
Jeremi Beam

GRAPHIC DESIGNERS
Brandi Etheredge
Katie Beth Shirley

ART DIRECTOR
Drew Francis

PUBLISHING ASSISTANTS
Lee Moore
Janie Walters